# The *Mary Celeste* Ghost Ship

by Anita Nahta Amin

CAPSTONE PRESS
a capstone imprint

Published by Capstone Press, an imprint of Capstone
1710 Roe Crest Drive, North Mankato, Minnesota 56003
capstonepub.com

Library of Congress Cataloging-in-Publication Data
Names: Amin, Anita Nahta, author.
Title: The Mary Celeste ghost ship / by Anita Nahta Amin.
Description: North Mankato, Minnesota : Capstone Press, 2022. | Series: History's
mysteries | Includes bibliographical references and index. | Audience: Ages 8-11 |
Audience: Grades 4-6 | Summary: "In 1872, the Mary Celeste merchant ship set sail
from New York, bound for Italy. About a month later, it was spotted adrift in the
ocean. The crew had vanished. The ship's charts were found scattered, and crew
members' belongings were still onboard. The lifeboat was missing. What happened
to the crew? Explore the theories behind the crew's disappearance and why it has
become one of history's greatest mysteries"-- Provided by publisher. Identifiers:
LCCN 2021023362 (print) | LCCN 2021023363 (ebook) | ISBN 9781663958754
(hardcover) | ISBN 9781666320640 (paperback) | ISBN 9781666320657 (pdf) | ISBN
9781666320671 (kindle edition) Subjects: LCSH: Mary Celeste (Brig)--Juvenile
literature. | Shipwrecks--Juvenile literature. | Disappearances (Parapsychology)--
Juvenile literature.
Classification: LCC G530.M37 A65 2022 (print) | LCC G530.M37 (ebook) |
DDC 910.9163/38--dc23
LC record available at https://lccn.loc.gov/2021023362
LC ebook record available at https://lccn.loc.gov/2021023363

Editorial Credits
Editor: Carrie Sheely; Designer: Kim Pfeffer; Media Researcher: Morgan Walters;
Production Specialist: Laura Manthe

Image Credits
Alamy: Chronicle, 11, 13, Historic Images, 18; Bridgeman Images: Look and Learn,
17, 21, Peter Newark American Pictures, 9; Getty Images: adoc-photos, top 27,
DeAgostini Picture Library, 5, Imagno, bottom 7, Keystone/Stringer, top 7, xavigm,
top 23; Shutterstock: Alexander Kondratenko, 14, Cmspic, 10, Daniel Eskridge,
bottom 27, Design Projects, 15, ialehsn, bottom 25, Ilya Brin, 19, Irina Kovancova, top
25, Melkor3D, Cover, ssuaphotos, bottom 23, welburnstuart, 28

# Table of Contents

Words in **bold** are in the glossary.

# INTRODUCTION

## A Ship Abandoned

Imagine you're walking down the street in New York in 1872. A newsboy thrusts a paper at you. The headline reads, "The *Mary Celeste* Found Abandoned at Sea–Entire Crew Missing." You gasp. The *Mary Celeste* was a sailing ship. It had set off from New York about a month ago. What had gone wrong?

The ship had never reached Italy. It had been found drifting near Portugal. Everyone on the ship was gone! Where was Captain Briggs? Where were his wife and child? Where was his crew? *Mary Celeste* had become a **ghost ship.**

Tragedy struck the *Mary Celeste* in 1872. Almost 150 years later, no one knows what happened to the people on the ship.

*Mary Celeste* had large sails to catch the wind.

# CHAPTER 1

# Gone Without a Trace

Captain Benjamin Briggs had a job to do. A company had hired him to take 1,701 barrels of alcohol to Italy. The trip across the Atlantic Ocean would be long and hard. But Briggs was prepared. He had sailed many times over the past 10 years.

On November 7, 1872, his ship, the *Mary Celeste,* left New York. On board were Briggs, his wife, Sarah, their 2-year-old daughter, Sophia, and seven crewmen.

The trip seemed doomed from the start. For a couple weeks, storms lashed at their ship. On November 25, the ship's **log** was updated with their location for the last time. They could see Santa Maria, an island near Portugal. Then something went wrong.

Benjamin Briggs was an experienced seaman and ship captain.

## Fact

New York was a very busy port in America in the 1800s. It served more ships than all other American ports total. Hundreds of ships were docked there each day.

Almost two weeks later, in early December, the ship *Dei Gratia* was sailing 400 miles (644 kilometers) east of Portugal. The captain, David Morehouse, saw the *Mary Celeste*. He knew Briggs and his family. The *Mary Celeste* should have reached Italy by now. Why was it here?

Morehouse sent some of his crew to check the *Mary Celeste*. They found the ship to be in sailing condition. But Briggs, his family, and the crew were missing.

## A Trail of Clues

The crew found clues on the *Mary Celeste*. Some sails were torn. Slashes were found in the ship. One of two pumps that removed water from the ship had been taken apart. The sounding rod was lying on the deck. The rod measured how much water was in a low part of the ship's body. The water that had seeped in was 3.5 feet (1 meter) high.

Crew from the *Dei Gratia* rowed toward *Mary Celeste* to see if anyone was on board.

## Fact

*Mary Celeste* was first named the *Amazon*. It was built in Canada in 1861.

Items were also missing. The lifeboat was gone. A rope hung off the back of the ship. Had this rope been tied to the lifeboat? The captain's papers and **navigation** tools were missing. Nine alcohol barrels were empty.

Jewelry, money, and personal items were still there. Ship charts were left in a mess. A stained sword was found too.

Morehouse had a crew member sail the *Mary Celeste* to Gibraltar. It arrived on December 13. Everyone wondered what had happened to the ship.

Gibraltar is a British territory that borders Spain to the north.

The table was reportedly set when the *Dei Gratia* crew boarded *Mary Celeste*.

# WAS THE *MARY CELESTE* DOOMED?

Over time, many sailors came to think the *Mary Celeste* was doomed. The first time it sailed in 1861, Captain Robert McLellan became sick and later died. Some captains had accidents, including crashing the ship onto rocks in a bad storm in 1867.

# CHAPTER 2

# Foul Play

Slashes in the ship. A stained sword. Some people wondered if the crew had met a violent ending.

In Gibraltar, Morehouse was a **suspect**. He wanted a reward for the *Mary Celeste*. If someone saved an abandoned boat, its owner had to pay a reward. Otherwise, the rescuer could keep the boat. Had Morehouse thrown everyone overboard to collect a **salvage payment**?

Some people doubt Morehouse's involvement. He and Briggs were said to be friends. The sword stains turned out to not be blood. The weather may have splintered the wooden railing and **bow**, making slashes. Murder couldn't be proven. Yet the court didn't seem to fully believe Morehouse. He got a reward of 1,700 pounds (about $8,500). This was only about one-fifth of the value of the ship and its cargo.

Soon after *Mary Celeste* was found, some people thought violence aboard the ship might have resulted in the crew members' deaths.

## Fact

The *Dei Gratia* had a job to take petroleum to Gibraltar. The ship left New York eight days after the *Mary Celeste*.

# Pirate Attack

Pirates roamed the waters off North Africa in the late 1800s. They attacked ships and stole cargo. They kidnapped people. Portugal and Gibraltar border these waters. Had pirates kidnapped the *Mary Celeste* crew? Some people thought so. But money and jewelry were still on the ship. No one had robbed it.

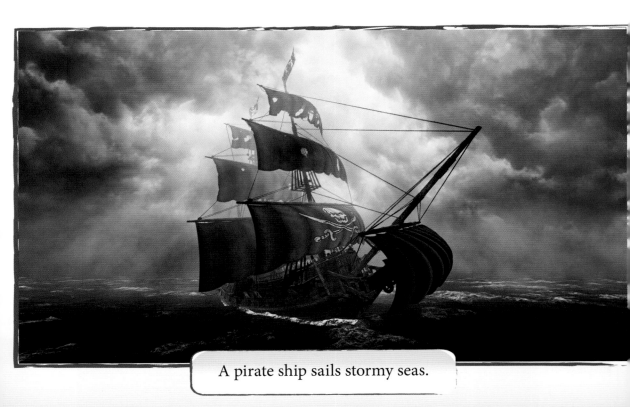

A pirate ship sails stormy seas.

# Mutiny

Another idea explaining the abandoned ship was that the crew committed **mutiny**. They could have attacked the Briggs family to take control of the *Mary Celeste*. Some people thought two brothers in the crew hurt Briggs. They didn't have any personal items on board. Was it because they didn't plan to stay? But their relative later explained they had lost everything in a prior shipwreck. Others question the mutiny idea. If the crew committed mutiny, why would they risk their lives leaving on a lifeboat?

Pirates sometimes brought their stolen goods to remote islands.

# A Get-Rich Plan

Several people, including Briggs, owned the *Mary Celeste.* He had spent his life savings to buy his share. The ship with its cargo was **insured** for $46,000. If all were lost in an accident, the insurance company might pay that much. Was the *Mary Celeste* crew hiding somewhere? Were they waiting to claim insurance money? Some people think Briggs and Morehouse worked together. Did Morehouse become greedy and hurt Briggs?

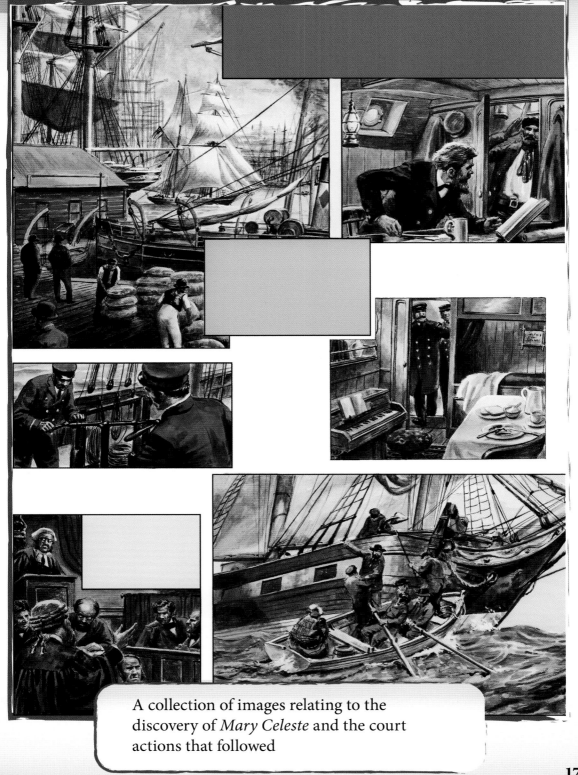

A collection of images relating to the discovery of *Mary Celeste* and the court actions that followed

Many people couldn't see the two friends committing a crime. Briggs wanted to retire from sailing. The extra money would have helped him. But Briggs had left his son, Arthur, back home. He was finishing school in the care of his grandmother. Would he leave without his son?

Investigators found few clues as to why *Mary Celeste* was found adrift.

In 1872, $46,000 was a lot of money. It would be like having about $1 million today!

The main investigator from Gibraltar, Frederick Solly-Flood, studied the clues for more than three months. He couldn't prove any kind of **foul play** was involved.

# CHAPTER 3

# Abandon Ship!

Was Captain Briggs worried the ship would sink? The sounding rod was on the deck. This tool measured 3.5 feet (1 m) of water flooding the bottom of the ship. But this wasn't enough water to sink the ship. With his sailing experience, Briggs likely would have known that.

Normally, water could be pumped out. But a pump had been taken apart. Was it broken? Workers had recently done construction work on the *Mary Celeste*. The ship had also carried coal on the last job. Coal dust and construction rubble could have clogged the pumps.

If they couldn't get water out, Briggs may have abandoned the ship, scared it would sink. They could see Santa Maria. They may have tried to row there for help but drowned on the way.

Briggs and the rest of the crew may have left *Mary Celeste* in the lifeboat if they felt their lives were in danger.

# Lost at Sea

When you're lost, you might check a map or ask someone for help. Maybe Captain Briggs had become lost.

Researchers checked the ship's log. They mapped where the *Mary Celeste* was on certain days. They found it was off course by 120 miles (193 km)!

Both the chronometer and sextant were missing when the ship was found. The chronometer kept track of time. The sextant measured the position of the sun, moon, or stars. Sailors used both tools to check charts and find their location. If the chronometer had the wrong time, they wouldn't know where they were. Santa Maria was the last stop for hundreds of miles. Did they try to row there in the lifeboat? Did bad weather cause them to drown on their way?

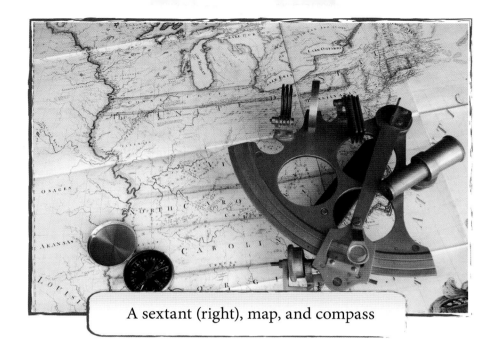

A sextant (right), map, and compass

# SHIP LOGS

The ship's log shows what a captain did on a trip. It acts as proof in case an accident or something unexpected happens. The log can include the time, direction, speed, weather, and location. The *Mary Celeste*'s last log entry was made at 5:00 a.m. on November 25. Its reported location in the log was about 500 miles (805 km) away from where Morehouse found it.

# Danger!

The *Mary Celeste*'s cargo was dangerous. Alcohol can catch fire or explode. The nine empty barrels were made of red oak. This type of wood leaks. Fumes from the leaked alcohol may have been strong. Maybe Briggs thought the ship was going to explode! Did he order everyone to **evacuate** to the lifeboat? Wind could have snapped the rope tying them to the ship. Did the ship sail away, leaving the crew to drown in rough waters?

Morehouse's crew didn't mention smelling any fumes, though. And the main hatch leading down to the alcohol was closed. Wouldn't an explosion have forced it open?

Some researchers think a fire started—maybe from barrels rubbing together or a lit pipe. There were no burn marks or ash. But research has shown an explosive fire can still happen with cool air behind it.

Barrels made of red oak are more likely to leak than those made of other kinds of wood.

Accidents aboard ships can cause explosions.

# CHAPTER 4

# Storms, Earthquakes, and More

Bad weather was common on the trip. The evening of November 24, another storm hit. Some people think a **waterspout** blew everyone overboard and they drowned. Others think an underwater earthquake struck. They're common near Portugal.

The shaking from a quake or a storm may have spilled alcohol from the barrels. Did Briggs want to evacuate the ship until the fumes passed? This would explain why their belongings were left behind. They planned to return but drowned before they could do so.

Some people think a bad storm could have caused the crew to fall overboard.

Others have suggested more far-fetched theories for what happened. Some say a sea monster attacked the ship. Sailors often told stories about attacking sea monsters in the 1800s. People have even said aliens snatched the crew. But these ideas are not widely believed.

A legendary sea monster called the kraken is said to use its many tentacles to bring down ships.

The answer to the *Mary Celeste* mystery is still lost at sea with the crew. Did Briggs order everyone off the ship after they became lost? Did a storm knock them overboard? Were they trying to escape danger? Did a crime occur? What do you think happened?

Today, what happened to *Mary Celeste*'s crew remains a mystery.

# Cold Case File

## The Main Theories

**1. They fled an alcohol fire or explosion.**

Afterward, bad weather caused them to drown in their lifeboat. Many people believe this theory.

**2. They feared the ship would sink and fled.**

The ship was taking on water, and the pumps weren't working. The crew fled to the lifeboat, and they drowned.

**3. They became lost after the chronometer failed.**

They then tried to row to Santa Maria for help. They drowned on the way.

**4. A waterspout blew the crew overboard and they drowned.**

**5. There was a plan to collect insurance money.**

Briggs and the crew might have tried to go into hiding but drowned. Or Morehouse could have been working with Briggs but then betrayed him.

**6. The crew died after pirates attacked.**

Many think this idea is unlikely. The ship wasn't robbed.

# Glossary

**bow** (BAU)—the front end of a ship

**evacuate** (i-VA-kyuh-wayt)—to leave an area during a time of danger

**foul play** (FOWL PLAY)—the use of physical force to cause injury or death

**ghost ship** (GOHST SHIP)—a ship found floating with no living crew aboard

**insure** (in-SHUR)—to enter into a contract where one agrees to guarantee another's item against loss or damage; if loss or damage occurs, money is paid to make up for the loss

**log** (LOG)—a written record of a ship's activities

**mutiny** (MYOOT-uh-nee)—a revolt against the captain of a ship

**navigation** (NAV-uh-gay-shuhn)—following a course point by point to get from one place to another

**salvage payment** (SAL-vij PAY-munt)—a reward paid for saving a ship or its cargo or for the lives and property rescued in a wreck

**suspect** (SUHSS-pekt)—someone who may be responsible for a crime

**waterspout** (WAW-tur-spaut)—a mass of spinning wind that stretches from a cloud to a body of water

# Read More

Gagne, Tammy. *Haunted Ships.* North Mankato, MN: Capstone, 2018.

Loh-Hagan, Virginia. *Mary Celeste.* Ann Arbor, MI: Cherry Lake Publishing, 2018.

Roland, James. *Frightful Ghost Ships.* Minneapolis: Lerner Publications, 2017.

# Internet Sites

*Abandoned Ship: The* Mary Celeste
smithsonianmag.com/history/abandoned-ship-the-mary-celeste-174488104/

*Academic Kids:* Mary Celeste
academickids.com/encyclopedia/index.php/Mary_Celeste

*Reader's Digest: 10 Ghost Ship Mysteries That Can't Be Explained*
rd.com/list/ghost-ships/

# Index

# Author Biography

Anita Nahta Amin is the author of children's books and short stories. She lives in Florida with her husband and twin children. She can often be found walking on the beach, watching the ships sail past. More information about her books can be found at www.AnitaAminBooks.com. She loves hearing from readers!